OUR FIVE SENSES

Taste

Sally Morgan

WAYLAND

Explore the world with **Popcorn** - your complete first non-fiction library.

Look out for more titles in the **Popcorn** range. All books have the same format of simple text and awesome images. Text is carefully matched to the pictures to help readers to identify and understand key vocabulary.
www.waylandbooks.co.uk/popcorn

Published in 2015 by Wayland
Copyright Wayland 2015

Wayland
Hachette Children's Books
338 Euston Road
London NW1 3BH

Wayland Australia
Level 17/207 Kent Street
Sydney NSW 2000

Editor: Nicola Edwards
Designer: Robert Walster
Picture Researcher: Shelley Noronha
Series consultant: Kate Ruttle
Design concept: Paul Cherrill

British Library Cataloguing in Publication Data
Morgan, Sally
Taste. - (Popcorn. Five senses)
1. Taste - Juvenile literature
I. Title
612.8'8
First published in 2009 by Wayland
ISBN: 978 0 7502 8890 3

Wayland is a division of Hachette Children's Books,
an Hachette UK company.
www.hachette.co.uk

Photographs:
Cover Dale Hogan/istock; title page Nina Matthews/istock; p4 Bananastock/Jupiter Media/ImagePick; p5 Comstock/Jupiter Media/ImagePick; p6 Dale Hogan/istock; p7 © M. Thomsen/zefa/Corbis; p8 Kasia Biel/istock; p9 Nina Shannon/ istock; p10 Andy Lim/Shutterstock; p11 Fritz Polking/Ecoscene; p12 © Gareth Brown/Corbis; p13 © Norbert Schaefer/CORBIS; p14 Shutterstock; p15 Martyn f. Chillmaid; p16 Nina Matthews/istock; p17 Ramona Heim/istock; p18 © Image Source/Corbis; p19 Anna Ziska/istock; p20 © Robert Harding World; p21 Rich Legg/istock; p22 Martyn f. Chillmaid; p23 (c) Dorling Kindersley

Contents

# Taste

We enjoy the food we eat because it is tasty. Imagine having to eat food every day that tasted of nothing.

Yum! Party foods taste good!

4

Taste is one of our five senses.
We taste food with our tongue.
When we chew food, the tongue
touches and tastes the food.

Yuck! Medicines usually don't taste very nice!

Our five
senses are
sight, hearing,
touch, smell
and taste.

Taste buds on the tongue

Have a look in a mirror at your tongue. It is covered with lots of bumps. These bumps help you to grip your food.

You use your tongue to move food around your mouth and to lick your lips.

6

The bumps are covered in taste buds.
Taste buds detect five flavours –
sweet, sour, bitter, salty and something
called umami (say oo-mah-mee),
a savoury taste.

There are about 10,000 taste buds on your tongue.

How do taste buds work?

Each taste bud is covered in very tiny hairs. When the hairs detect a flavour they send a message to the brain.

Chillis give food a hot taste.

The hot taste of chilli is really a feeling of pain on the tongue.

It is difficult to taste if you have a dry mouth. When you chew food you produce saliva. Saliva helps you to taste and swallow your food.

A cold drink stops the taste buds from working so you cannot taste food so well.

Animals and taste

Many animals have more taste buds than people. This gives them a much better sense of taste.

A catfish has taste buds all over its body.

Catfish have ten times more taste buds than people.

Some animals, such as bears, taste with their tongue, as we do. Others taste with other parts of their bodies, such as their feet or tentacles.

The butterfly has hairs on its feet to taste leaves.

Sweet and sour

Do you like the taste of biscuits, cakes and fizzy fruit drinks? They contain sugar which makes them taste sweet.

Cakes are made with sugar and may have a sugary topping, too.

Sour foods are sharp, acid-tasting foods. Lemon juice, rhubarb and vinegar have a sour taste.

A grapefruit is a sour-tasting fruit.

Bitter and salty

Some tastes, such as coffee and dark chocolate, are bitter. Many children do not like foods with a bitter taste.

Umami is a savoury taste that is found in Chinese and Japanese foods.

Fish and other seafoods have a naturally salty taste. Some foods, for example, crisps and bacon, have salt added to them.

Some people sprinkle salt over food to make it more tasty.

Too much salt is bad for your health.

Smell and taste

When you put food in your mouth, its smell enters your nose from the back of your mouth. The smell of the food helps you to identify its taste.

Your senses of smell and taste work together when you eat.

When your sense of smell isn't working well, such as when you have a cold, it makes it harder for you to taste things.

When you have a cold you may sneeze a lot and your nose can become blocked.

Protecting your body

Your sense of taste can protect you. Often a food that is not safe to eat has a bad taste. When you put it in your mouth, its horrible taste makes you spit it out.

Milk that has gone off has a nasty smell and a sour taste.

When the weather's hot, or when we exercise, our bodies sweat. Sweat contains water and salt. We have to eat and drink to replace them.

Exercising makes us thirsty.

Supertasters

Supertasters are people who have many more taste buds than other people.
They can taste the tiniest flavours in food.

Supertasters can detect many different flavours in various types of tea.

Supertasters often do not enjoy bitter foods, such as coffee or spinach, because they are very sensitive to this taste.

A good sense of taste is very important for people who work as chefs.

More women are supertasters than men.

Your sense of taste

Try this taste test and see which breads you like.

Drink a sip of water and then take a small piece of bread. Feel the texture and then smell it. Now eat it. What flavours can you taste? Do this for each of the different breads, taking a sip of water first to remove the taste of other breads.

Which bread had the strongest flavour? Which bread did you like the most? Which bread did you like the least?

Confusing the taste buds

You will need:

• some slices of different foods, such as apple, orange, cheese, onion and potato.

Smell and taste are closely linked and it is easy to confuse your taste buds.

First close your eyes, hold your nose and try tasting a slice of each of the different foods. Don't swallow the foods you've tasted – spit them out into a paper towel. Try to work out what each of the foods is. Can you taste the difference between a slice of apple and a slice of potato?

Now, hold a slice of orange under your nose and eat a piece of apple. What does the apple taste like? Try this with the other foods.

Glossary

acid a sharp, sour taste. Vinegar and lemon juice have an acid taste

brain the control centre of the body, found inside the head

saliva liquid produced in the mouth when you chew food

senses functions of the body through which we gather information about our surroundings

sensitive able to feel or detect something

supertaster someone who has more taste buds than usual, and a very good sense of taste

taste bud tiny bumps with hairs on the surface of the tongue that detect flavours

umami a savoury taste found in Chinese and Japanese foods

Index